Mess, Mercy, and Miracles

Finding God's Purpose in Every Season of Life

Heide Watson

ISBN: 9798993385327
Printed in the United States of America

Cover design by Heide Watson
First Edition

Mess, Mercy, and Miracles

Finding God's Purpose in Every Season of Life

A Devotional Journey by Heide Watson

About Author

I'm just a simple woman who has walked through her share of struggles, mistakes, and seasons of healing. Along the way, I've learned that God can take even the hardest parts of our story and use them for good.

My writing is real and raw because life is real and raw. These words come out of lessons I've lived, moments that broke me down, and the hope I found when God lifted me back up.

I don't write as someone who has it all figured out. I write as someone still on the journey—someone who knows what it feels like to be lost, lonely, and unsure, but also someone who has experienced God's grace in powerful ways.

If my words can help even one person feel less alone or remind them that God isn't finished with their story yet, then I know I'm walking in my purpose.

This is me—open, honest, and still learning every day. I'm grateful you're here, and I pray you find encouragement, truth, and hope in these pages.

Turning life's messes into
messages of hope through
God's love.

Preface

Life is messy. We all know what it feels like to walk through seasons that break us down—heartache, struggles, unanswered questions, or just the quiet weight of disappointment. Maybe that's where you are right now. Maybe you've been there before.

This devotional wasn't written to give you perfect answers or a polished picture of faith. It was written to remind you that you're not alone. That even in the hardest moments, God is present. That He takes the broken pieces and weaves them into something beautiful.

What you'll find in these pages are honest reflections— lessons learned the hard way, moments of God's grace that caught me by surprise, and reminders to keep holding on when life feels heavy. My prayer is that as you read, you'll find yourself nodding along, maybe even whispering, "That's me. I've felt that too."

This book is less about me and more about what God wants to show you. It's about finding hope in unexpected places. It's about remembering that your story matters. And it's about trusting that no season is wasted when God is writing the chapters.

So, take your time here. Breathe. Be honest with yourself. Let these words encourage you, challenge you, and point you back to the One who promises that your future still holds hope.

You are not forgotten. You are deeply loved. And you still have a purpose. And that's why this devotional is built around five core truths to carry you through every season of life: God turns mess into message, stop comparing, slow down, self-worth in Christ, and purpose in every season.

With love and faith,
Heide Watson

TABLE OF CONTENTS

Section 1

MESS

Brokenness, Struggles, and Searching

Life doesn't spare any of us from hardship. We all know what it feels like to walk through seasons that strip us bare – moments where we question our worth, our purpose, even our faith. These are the times when brokenness feels louder than hope.

But here's the truth: God never wastes a mess. In fact, it's often in our lowest seasons that He begins His deepest work. These devotionals are about those raw, honest moments – when life feels heavy, but God is still whispering, "I am with you

Remember You Have a Purpose

My Story

There are days when I find myself in a slump—feeling low, defeated, even questioning my purpose. Maybe you've been there too. Those moments can feel heavy, like nothing will ever change.

For me, one of those seasons came when everything I was trying seemed to fall flat. I was pouring into people, working hard, showing up, but still getting nowhere and feeling invisible. I felt I could never get ahead financially; life was throwing me curve balls constantly. My energy was depleted. I remember sitting in my car after a long day, staring at the steering wheel, thinking, does any of this even matter? Does my life matter? Do I matter to anyone?

Here I was putting all this time and energy into everyone else, but I was empty, stressed, drained, feeling unloved…

That night, I opened my Bible just looking for something – anything to hold on to. It hit me that I had been trying to seek my worth by how someone else treated me or how successful I looked. I was focused on how people noticed me, and I was looking for love in all the wrong places. But God wasn't asking me to prove myself – He was asking me to trust Him and walk in the purpose He had already placed inside me.

The truth is, we aren't here by accident. God placed us on this earth for His purpose – to serve, to love, and to share His truth with others. Even when life feels pointless, His plan is still at work in us.

I realized that night I needed to focus on learning to love myself and find happiness in helping others. I needed to stop focusing on what others were not giving me and focus on what God has placed in me.

"The world still needs the gift God placed inside you."

So tomorrow, when you wake up, remember this: it's not time to give up. There are lives only you can touch. Hearts only you can influence. Stories only you can share.

So get up. Breathe deep. Speak to God. Know that He is with you through it all, and He will carry you when you feel like you can't carry yourself.

And in case no one has told you today—let me remind you:
You are worthy.
You are loved.
You are beautiful.

Scripture says, "I can do all this through him who gives me strength." (Philippians 4:13). You don't have to muster up the strength on your own. God has already promised to supply it.

Your life has a purpose. Don't give up—God placed a gift inside you that this world still needs.

Prayer

Father, thank You for reminding me that my life has meaning and purpose. On the days when I feel low or defeated, help me to remember that You are with me. Strengthen me to get back up, to keep moving forward, and to use the gifts You've given me to touch the lives You've placed in my path. In Jesus' name, Amen.

Remember You Have a Purpose

Devotional Guide

Scripture: Jeremiah 29:11

"For I know the plans I have for you," declares the Lord, "plans to prosper you and not to harm you, plans to give you hope and a future."

Devotional

Have you ever had a morning where getting out of bed felt impossible? Where the weight of yesterday's mistakes or today's worries made you question why you should even try? I've been there more times than I can count.

But here's what Jeremiah 29:11 reminds me: God's plans are not accidental. They are intentional. He doesn't just allow us to exist—He places us here on purpose, for a purpose. And not a vague, "maybe someday" kind of purpose. A personal one, crafted specifically for you.

The enemy loves to whisper lies that we're worthless, replaceable, or that our lives don't matter. But think about it—why would God promise hope and a future if your life wasn't valuable to Him? Why would He place a gift inside you if He didn't intend for you to use it?

Your purpose might not be flashy or loud. It might be something as simple as showing kindness to someone who's hurting, raising children to know God, or listening to a friend when no one else will. But don't underestimate the eternal impact of those seemingly small things. When we feel defeated, it's usually because we're comparing our story to someone else's. But God didn't call you to live their life—He called you to live yours. The world doesn't need another version of them; it needs the one-of-a-kind version of you.

So tomorrow morning, when you wake up, remind yourself: It's not time to give up. The world still needs the light God put inside of you. There are lives only you can reach, hearts only you can influence, and stories only you can tell.

Story

I once went through a season where I felt invisible—like nothing I did mattered. Then one night, I came across a video that a lady said, "You may not see your purpose yet, but someone else sees God shining through you." That reminder kept me going. Sometimes we underestimate the impact we're already making.

Takeaway Line

Your purpose isn't lost—it's alive, waiting for you to walk in it.

Reflection

What unique gift or passion has God placed in you that the world still needs?

Practical Step

Write down three things you've done this week that brought light to someone else, no matter how small. That's God working through you.

Prayer

Lord, remind me each day that I am here for a purpose. Help me stop comparing myself to others and start walking boldly in the calling You've given me. Give me the courage to shine my light in a world that desperately needs hope. Amen.

With Love,
Heide Watson

Maybe Right Now

My Story

God had whispered this lesson to me before, but this season it became clearer than ever. And truthfully, it's a lesson I've had to wrestle with more than once – as I'm sure many of you have too.

Not long ago, I watched a sermon that pierced straight to my heart. The pastor said something simple yet powerful: "Be at peace with the season you're in." He reminded us that sometimes the struggles we face are not punishments but invitations – opportunities to trust God more deeply and to lean into His love instead of our own strength.

As he spoke, I drifted back to a night when I sat alone in my bedroom, scrolling endlessly on my phone. Picture after picture filled the screen – smiling couples, dream vacations, celebrations, perfect homes. Everyone else looked like they were living the life I longed for. And in that moment a thought cut deep. If I disappeared tomorrow, would anyone even notice? The weight of it broke me. Tears fell as I whispered, "God, what's wrong with me?'

And it was in that raw moment – in the quiet, in the ache - that His presence met me. Not with fireworks. Not with thunder. But with a gentle whisper that settled in my spirit. "I am His, His love is enough for me." That night, I began to understand. God's love doesn't just cover us in crisis; it fills the emptiness where our hearts are starving for validation.

From that moment, I knew I had to stop comparing myself to others. What I was seeing online wasn't the whole truth, it was the highlight reel. Behind every smiling picture could be an untold struggle. The problem wasn't them; it was me. I had to confront why I was so unhappy with myself.

So often we look for completion in other people. We seek validation, affection, or someone to rescue us. But no person can fill the hole only God's love was designed to fill. When His love takes root, something shifts. We begin to see ourselves the way He sees us, and that opens the door to healthier self-love and genuine connection with others.

That truth has been central to my journey. It's why I've written about self-love repeatedly, and why I started a women's Facebook group called Women Who Motivate Other Women. I wanted a space where women could lift each other up, speak life instead of competition, and remind each other that we are not alone.

Still, I've noticed a common misunderstanding: people often confuse self-love with selfishness. But true self-love is not arrogance, it's agreement with God's view of us. He made us with purpose, with intention, with beauty woven into our very being. Imagine standing before the Maker of oceans, sunsets, stars and saying, "You got it wrong with me." Impossible. Everything He creates carries His mark of beauty – including you.

"Self-love is not selfish—it's seeing yourself the way God sees you."

Yet even when we know this, life's valleys test us. Depression or discouragement creeps in, and the questions come: Am I comparing again? Am I expecting someone else to fix me? Am I clinging to relationships because I fear being alone? These questions sting, but they are the starting line of healing. Change begins when we say, I am the one responsible for my own heart work. Healing isn't tidy. There are nights when loneliness echoes and tears soak the pillow. Thoughts whisper, No one loves me. I'll always be alone. I've learned not to run from those thoughts, but to treat them like signals, an alarm calling me back to God. Sometimes that looks like journaling, sometimes prayer, sometimes simply opening my Bible and talking with Him like a friend. And often, I discover the root of my pain runs deeper than I expected – sometimes the wounds I didn't even realize were still open.

Another lesson? Not everyone will understand when you start working on yourself. Some will assume you're pulling away. Others may think you've changed. But this season isn't about pleasing them—it's about you and God. It's about rediscovering what brings you joy, what makes you laugh, what stirs peace in your soul. That's where true healing begins.

And healing, is not a one-time event. It's a journey you revisit, again and again. One simple tool that has anchored me in my journey is asking, "Am I aware?" When negativity starts to spiral, I whisper that question until my heart steadies in the present. Not lost in yesterday. Not worried about tomorrow. Just here – right now. I first learned this practice through Life Coach Mandy Morris in her Authentic Living Program, and it continues to center me.

And please remember, don't be fooled by social media. What we see online is never the whole picture. Even those who seem to "have it all" – money, fame, influence – carry battles we never see. None of those things bring lasting joy. True peace comes only from God and from embracing the way He designed us.

So, if you feel unseen, unloved, or overlooked in this season, hear this: maybe right now is the moment God is calling you back. Back to Him. Back to yourself. Lean in. Trust the process. Don't give up. You're here for a reason. You have a purpose.

And here's the bigger picture: when we learn to see ourselves through God's eyes, we naturally begin to see others through His eyes too. Healing in us becomes healing through us. The love He pours in spills out, sparking encouragement, hope, and even healing in others.

"See what great love the Father has lavished on us, that we should be called children of God! And that is what we are." — 1 John 3:1

God's love is enough to sustain you in every season. When you embrace His love, you learn to love yourself and others more genuinely.

Prayer

Father, thank You for a love that never wavers. Teach me to see myself the way You see me – fearfully, wonderfully, and intentionally made. When I'm tempted to compare, to doubt, or to search for validation elsewhere, remind me that Your love is enough. Give me peace in this season, courage for the process, and faith to trust You with what I cannot see. In Jesus' name, Amen.

Maybe Right Now

Devotional Guide

Scripture: Psalm 34:18

"The Lord is close to the brokenhearted and saves those who are crushed in spirit."

Devotional

Maybe right now your heart feels heavy. Maybe you're carrying disappointment, loneliness, or fear. If so, you're not alone.

Psalm 34:18 promises us something powerful: God isn't distant from pain—He draws close to it. He leans in when our hearts are breaking. When the world feels like it's falling apart, He whispers, "I'm here. You're not alone."

We often think healing has to come in giant leaps, but sometimes it comes in quiet moments. A prayer whispered through tears. A sunrise after a sleepless night. A friend's encouragement at just the right time.

Maybe right now, all God is asking of you is to let Him in. To trust Him enough to sit in your pain with Him, instead of trying to carry it alone. Healing begins there.

Story

During one of my hardest seasons, a pastor reminded me that "right now" is where God often works the most. Not in the someday, not in the when-it's-fixed—right here in the middle of the mess.

Takeaway Line
God meets you in the "right now," even when it feels like rock bottom.

Reflection

What pain or struggle do you need to invite God into right now?

Practical Step

Pause today and thank God for one small blessing in your present moment, no matter how heavy life feels.

Prayer

Lord, thank You for being close to the brokenhearted. Help me to feel Your presence in my hurt and give me the courage to trust You with the healing process. Amen.

With Love,
Heide Watson

John 14:27 – Peace in the Storm

My Story

What looks like "bad" isn't always bad—it's shaping us, teaching. This past year has been the hardest of my life. I'm not ashamed to say it. Every area of my world felt like it collapsed at once. Tonight was my breaking point.

The day had actually started well. My dad had surgery to get a pacemaker, and it went perfectly. My parents informed me they were giving me a new puppy, a Goldendoodle. This was to help with my empty nest because my only child was graduating High School and moving off to college. Things felt good today for a change. I was hopeful, ready for new beginnings. I thought, this is my year. 2022, here I come.

But on the drive home, a text message came through. Just like that, all the peace I'd been holding onto slipped away. Isn't it crazy how one small thing can trigger every doubt, insecurity, and fear we thought we'd buried? By the time I got home, I was in tears—ugly tears. The kind where your face swells and your chest feels like it can't breathe. I felt completely done. Out of options. Beaten.

And that's when I realized: I had no choice but to give it to God. I had been trying to control everything on my own strength for several years, but my strength was gone. I did everything in my power to handle this situation and try to control it on my own. Nothing was working. Every time I saw some relief, I was hit by another storm right after the other.

I've heard it said that the devil doesn't want us closer to God, and that's why the attacks intensify. I believe that's true. But I also believe sometimes the Holy Spirit allows challenges to refine us, pushing us to rely on God instead of ourselves.

Looking back, I can see how much of my life was spent trying to find myself in the eyes of others—family, friendships, relationships. I was living for how people saw me, not for who God made me to be. Every relationship, every friendship, every trial—I grew from them. But I was still stubborn, still holding on to control.

So that night, sitting in my car, sobbing, I finally broke. I let it all go. I told God, "I can't fix this anymore. I've tried. I've done everything in my power. It's Yours."

"The very day I let go, God stepped in and took control."

Within hours, the situation shifted. It wasn't me. It wasn't my doing. It was God. After years of fighting to prove I was strong enough, He waited patiently until I finally surrendered. Then He fixed it—just like that.

Not long after, another text came through. It simply said: John 14:27.

I opened my Bible and read:

"Peace I leave with you; my peace I give you. I do not give to you as the world gives. Do not let your hearts be troubled and do not be afraid."

This verse had carried me before, but in the storm it became more than words – it became my anchor.

I broke again—but this time in gratitude. That very day, everything changed. The problem that had weighed me down, the one I kept trying to fix on my own, was lifted. All my stressing and striving couldn't do what God did in an instant. He stepped in, took control, and handled it far better than I ever could.

Friends, it is hard to let go of control. It feels vulnerable. It feels weak. But peace doesn't come from us holding everything together. It comes from Jesus. He has it under control. Always.

So whatever battle you're fighting—give it to Him. Trust Him. Be at peace. He will not fail you.

"Cast all your anxiety on him because he cares for you." — 1 Peter 5:7

"Be still, and know that I am God." — Psalm 46:10

Prayer

Father, I've tried to carry so much on my own. Forgive me for the times I've clung to control instead of trusting You. Teach me to let go, to hand You the battles I cannot win in my own strength. Fill me with Your peace—the kind only You can give. Thank You for stepping in, for working in ways I could never manage on my own. I surrender it all to You. In Jesus' name, Amen.

"In some of my other devotionals, I'll share how God even used the messiest parts of my story to reveal His grace."

John 14:27 – Peace in the Storm

Devotional Guide

Scripture: John 14:27 (NIV)

"Peace I leave with you; my peace I give you. I do not give to you as the world gives. Do not let your hearts be troubled and do not be afraid."

Devotional

Life can change in an instant. One text message. One phone call. One unexpected turn. Suddenly peace feels like it's gone.

But here's the truth: peace isn't something the world can give—or take away. Jesus offers a peace that isn't tied to circumstances. His peace steadies us when everything else shakes.

The night I finally surrendered control of my struggles, I realized something: I had been holding onto peace like it was mine to protect. But Jesus never asked me to guard it—He asked me to receive it.

Surrendering is scary. It feels like weakness. But in reality, surrender is the doorway to strength. The moment we hand it over, Jesus steps in and whispers, "Be still. I've got this."

Story

I'll never forget sitting in my car, crying after a hard day, when I whispered, "Lord, I can't do this anymore." At that moment, peace washed over me—not because the problem disappeared, but because I knew I wasn't alone.

Takeaway Line

Peace doesn't mean the storm stops—it means you're steady in the middle of it.

Reflection

What storm in your life right now needs God's peace more than your control?

Practical Step

When anxiety rises, read John 14:27 aloud and breathe slowly until the words settle in your spirit.

Prayer

Jesus, I surrender my fears to You. Replace my anxiety with Your peace. Calm my spirit and remind me that You are in control. Amen.

With Love,
Heide Watson

Loving My Mess

My Story

God had already started showing me this lesson before, but in this season He pulled me deeper into it.

I remember a time when I was pouring myself into everyone else's problems. If someone needed me, I showed up. If someone called, I answered. Before I knew it, I was drained, exhausted, and resentful…

After that breaking point, I began to see my past differently. What once felt like a pile of failures started to look more like steppingstones God had used to grow me. My story wasn't ruined—it was being rewritten. That's why I can honestly say today: I love my mess because God used it.

For so long—going all the way back to childhood—I made one bad decision after another. Looking back now, I shake my head and wonder, what was I thinking? The truth is, I wasn't. And as an adult, the weight of those choices hit harder.

But here's the thing: all those choices shaped me into the woman I am today. Without them, I wouldn't have grown. I wouldn't be able to encourage others in their struggles. I wouldn't be who God is using me to be right now. So, as strange as it sounds, I am thankful for the mess.

Some of you know parts of my story, some don't. One of the things I've carried the most shame for is this: I've been married multiple times. People sometimes make remarks. Others look at me as if I'm "damaged goods," or assume I can't hold down a stable marriage or relationship for that matter. It stings. But what they don't know are the real reasons, the struggles, the lessons buried in each relationship. Of course I don't owe anyone an explanation, yet I often try to share in hopes they'll understand me better. Which takes me back to another devotion I wrote about, "Slow Down." (This example here is where I am in the other person's shoes wanting to be heard, yet no one wants to listen. Kind of ironic how life plays out at times). When I start to tell my story, sometimes it goes in one ear and out the other. Still, I've learned to smile through it.

Am I proud of my past? No. Would I change it? Also no. Every part of my story has taught me something. The problem is, rarely are we taught about love and marriage at 18. I wasn't aware what a healthy relationship was supposed to be like. We're told what not to do, but rarely taught what real love, support, and commitment look like. I did the best I knew how and immature at that.

Through every mistake and heartbreak, I've learned this: take the bad and find the good in it. Ask, what is the lesson here? How can I use this to move forward to grow?

"My past is not my shame—it's my testimony."

Maybe your life feels like a mess right now. Try making a list of the good things that came from it. Apply them to today. Stop beating yourself up for the past—it's gone. The only direction left is forward. Talk to God before making decisions. Trust Him to guide you into something better.

Recently, I've been walking closely with a friend who is healing from deep hurts. It's been a hard road for them, but healing is happening. Growth is happening. I prayed this morning in their home for God to ease their thoughts, to guide them, and to help me be the friend they need.

Life is messy, but it doesn't stay that way forever. Even at our lowest, we can still pull something good out of it.

Maybe today is your messy season. But tomorrow can be your glow-up. The new you. The healed you.

I love my mess because God used it. He forgave me, redeemed me, and gave me hope. And if He can do that for me, He can do it for you too.

"And we know that in all things God works for the good of those who love him, who have been called according to his purpose." — Romans 8:28

Your past isn't wasted—it's a testimony of God's grace.

Prayer

Father, thank You for using even the messiest parts of my story for good. Help me release the shame of the past and embrace it as testimony of Your forgiveness and redemption. Teach me to keep moving forward, trusting that You are writing a greater story through my life. In Jesus' name, Amen.

Loving My Mess

Devotional Guide

Scripture: Romans 8:28

"And we know that in all things God works for the good of those who love Him, who have been called according to His purpose."

Devotional

For much of my life, I looked back at my choices and thought, what on earth was I thinking? From childhood mistakes to adult missteps, I carried shame over the "mess" I had made. And yet, when I look at who I am today, I see that every single part of that journey shaped me into the woman I've become.

The truth is, God doesn't waste anything. Not even our mess. Every heartbreak, every poor decision, every broken relationship has been used to teach me, to refine me, and—most importantly—to draw me closer to Him. Life is messy. But within the mess, there are lessons.

Healing. Growth. Redemption. If you're in a messy season right now, don't despise it. Ask God, what do You want me to learn from this? How are You shaping me through this?

Remember: the same God who created beauty from dust can bring beauty from your brokenness.

Story

I used to carry shame for all my failed relationships and mistakes, feeling like they disqualified me from real love. But then I realized: God doesn't waste our mess. Every heartbreak, every wrong turn was shaping me into who I am today—and equipping me to encourage others in their own journeys.

Takeaway Line

Your mess doesn't disqualify you—God can turn it into your ministry.

Reflection

What is one "mess" from your past that God might be using to grow you or help others today?

Practical Step

Think of one lesson you've learned from a painful season. Share it with someone who might need encouragement right now.

Prayer

Lord, thank You for loving me in the middle of my mess. Help me release shame, embrace the lessons, and trust that You are working all things for my good. Amen.

With Love,
Heide Watson

Protect Your Energy

My Story

This reminder wasn't new, but God had to press it into me again so I wouldn't forget it. If you haven't noticed yet… I'm kind of stubborn and it obviously takes a lot for me to learn my lesson(s) in life…

Recently this question has been on my mind: "Why people who seem selfish sometimes look like they're thriving?"

I've asked myself that so many times. Maybe you have too. On the surface, it looks like people who cut corners or live only for themselves are prospering, while those who try to live right are left struggling. It can feel unfair.

I remember a season in my own life when I was constantly pouring myself into other people. If someone needed help, I was there. If someone had a problem, I tried to fix it. At first, it felt good to be the one people could count on. But over time, I noticed a pattern: certain people only came around when they needed something. They weren't calling to check on me, they weren't there to lift me up – they just wanted and wanted. Every conversation left me feeling smaller, emptier, more drained.

One night I came home after running around all day, and I just collapsed on my couch. I stared at the ceiling and realized: I was exhausted, but not just my body – my spirit was tired too. I had been giving, but nobody was pouring anything back into me. I was surrounded by energy vampires – people who drained me but never filled me.

Depression began seeping in. Thoughts of suicide were already on the table. My life was in a complete mess during this time with everything going on, yet I had no one that was pouring into me. I had no one to talk to or that would really listen to me. Trust me, I tried to have conversations. I bet you are reading this right now thinking "I've been there. No one seems to care."

To be real and raw with you, I came close to suicide twice. But there was something pulling at me saying "You have more to offer."

It became all too much for me to handle plus everything I had going on in my own personal life.

God got my attention.

That's when God started showing me something: the people I thought were "getting ahead" weren't doing anything magical. They were focused on themselves. They weren't giving their energy away to everyone else—they were channeling it into their own lives, their own goals, their own desires. And while that might look like blessings, it isn't the whole story.

Meanwhile, I was giving so much away that I was empty. And God never asked me to live empty. His Word says, "Above all else, guard your heart, for everything you do flows from it." (Proverbs 4:23). Everything. If my heart was tired, bitter, or burned out, then that's what was flowing into my relationships and my life.

I thought about the story of Mary and Martha (Luke 10:38–42). Martha was busy running around, serving, and trying to do it all—just like I was. Mary, on the other hand, sat at Jesus' feet, soaking in His presence. Martha grew frustrated because it felt like she was doing all the work. But Jesus gently told her that Mary had chosen the better part. That story reminds me that being filled comes before pouring out. Connection with God always comes before serving others.

And then I remembered Jesus Himself—how often He withdrew from the crowds to pray (Luke 5:16). If even the Son of God needed to step away, recharge, and reconnect with His Father, how much more do we?

That realization changed me. I learned that helping people is good, but helping from a place of emptiness is not. I needed to guard my heart, protect my energy, and let God refill me daily. Because when I'm filled with His peace and strength, what I give to others is so much better—healthier, stronger, and lasting.

So, here's what I've come to believe:
Protecting your energy isn't selfish. It's wisdom.
Guarding your heart doesn't mean shutting people out—it means keeping God at the center.
Loving others doesn't mean draining yourself—it means pouring from the overflow of God's Spirit in you.

Your energy is yours. Guard it. Focus it. Use it for good. Use it for Him.

Our energy—our attention, time, and emotional strength—is powerful. And where we place it matters.

When you let God fill you first, your love for others flows stronger, purer, and without regret.

Prayer

Father, thank You for reminding me that even Jesus needed to step away and be refilled. Teach me to guard my heart like Your Word says, to sit at Your feet like Mary did, and to find my strength in You before I give it to others. Help me to set healthy boundaries, to love wisely, and to live from a place of peace. In Jesus' name, Amen.

Protect Your Energy

Devotional Guide

Scripture: Proverbs 4:23

"Above all else, guard your heart, for everything you do flows from it."

Devotional

Ever notice how people who seem selfish sometimes look like they're thriving? Meanwhile, the ones always giving, pouring out, and sacrificing end up drained. It's because energy—our attention, time, and emotional strength—is powerful. And where we place it matters.

God calls us to love others, yes. But He also calls us to steward our lives wisely. You cannot pour from an empty cup. Protecting your energy doesn't mean being cold or unkind. It means choosing where and who you invest in.

If you're constantly worried about everyone else's life, you're fueling their growth while neglecting your own. But when you focus on what God has called you to do, and you give your energy to people who multiply joy instead of draining it, you begin to flourish.

Protect your energy. Not for selfishness, but for faithfulness.

Story

There was a time when I gave all my energy away trying to fix others, worrying about their lives more than my own. It left me drained. Then I realized: I can love people without letting them drain me. Protecting my energy doesn't make me selfish; it makes me healthy.

Takeaway Line

You don't have to give your energy to everyone—just the ones God places in your path.

Reflection

Are you giving your energy to people and things that drain you—or to what God has actually called you to?

Practical Step

Do a quick "energy check" today. Write down who leaves you feeling refreshed and who leaves you drained. Pray for wisdom to spend more time with the ones who lift you up.

Prayer

Father, give me wisdom to guard my heart and to invest my energy in what brings life, not in what steals peace. Amen.

With Love,
Heide Watson

Overlooked But Called

My Story

In life, we assume that when God gives us a dream, the people closest to us would be the first to recognize it, support it, and celebrate it. After all, they had walked through life with us. They know our struggles, our tears, and our prayers. Surely, they would be the ones cheering us on when God starts opening doors. Right?

But what I've learned was very different. Sometimes the people you expect to build you up are the ones who stay silent – or worse, dismiss what God is doing in your life. I'll never forget a time when I poured my heart into something I felt called to do. It wasn't just a hobby or a passing idea – I truly believed God had placed it on my heart. I was nervous to share it, but I thought, "This is my moment. They're going to be proud of me."

When I finally opened up, I expected excitement, encouragement, maybe even celebration. Instead, what I got was a shrug. A quick change of subject. Almost like what I had shared didn't matter at all. My chest tightened, and I remember thinking, "Did they even hear me? Do they even care?" The silence spoke louder than words.

Sometimes silence from the people closest to you is God's way of turning up the volume on His own voice.

For days afterward, I replayed that moment in my head. I questioned myself: "Maybe I'm not cut out for this. Maybe this isn't really from God. If the people who know me best don't believe in me, why should I?" Their lack of support dug deep into my confidence and left me wondering if I had misunderstood my calling altogether.

But then, something surprising happened. Later on, I mentioned that very project to someone online I never even met. They didn't know me well, didn't know my past, and had no reason to flatter me. Yet their reaction was completely different. They began speaking words of encouragement I didn't even know I needed. They reminded me that my story mattered, that my voice carried weight, and that God had a purpose for what I was doing. And then – right there – I knew and prayed.

I felt this sense come over me knowing that God sent encouragement to me through complete strangers. Even if it didn't come from places I expected. His plan for me doesn't depend on their applause.

That moment changed me. It didn't take away the sting of being overlooked by those I loved, but it gave me perspective. It showed me that my worth, my calling, and my purpose aren't defined by who supports me. They're defined by God alone. And if He has called me to it, He will equip me for it – even if He has to send strangers to remind me along the way.

"So do not fear, for I am with you; do not be dismayed, for I am your God. I will strengthen you and help you; I will uphold you with my righteous right hand." – Isaiah 41:10

Prayer

Lord, You know how much it hurts when the people I love the most don't see or celebrate what You are doing in my life. You know the sting of silence and the weight of disappointment. But You also remind me that my worth doesn't come from their words – it comes from Yours. Thank You for sending encouragement in unexpected places, and for always reminding me that I am seen, known, and called by You. Help me to keep moving forward in confidence, not because others cheer for me, but because You have already chosen me. In Jesus' name, Amen.

Overlooked But Called

Devotional Guide

Scripture: Mark 6:4

"A prophet is honored everywhere except in his own hometown and among his relatives and his own family."

Devotional

The silence of people we love can wound deeply. We expect their encouragement to fuel us, but often we're met with doubt or dismissal instead. Even Jesus experienced this. When He returned to His hometown of Nazareth, the people who knew Him best could not see Him as anything more than "the carpenter's son" (Matthew 13:55). Familiarity blinded them to His identity, and they rejected Him.

Jesus wasn't the only one. Joseph's brothers didn't celebrate his God – given dreams – they sold him into slavery (Genesis 37:19-20). David's father didn't even consider him worth presenting when Samuel came to anoint the king (1 Samuel 16:11). These stories remind us: lack of support doesn't mean lack of calling.

Sometimes God allows us to face silence so we learn to depend on His voice above every other. His Word becomes our affirmation:
* "For I know the plans I have for you," declares the Lord… (Jeremiah 29:11).
* "You are a chosen people, a royal priesthood, a holy nation, God's special possession…" (1 Peter 2:9).
* "For we are God's handiwork, created in Christ Jesus to do good works…" (Ephesians 2:20).

When human applause fades, these truths remind us: our value, our purpose, and our calling come from Him.

Takeaway Line

When the people closest to you don't recognize your calling, don't lose heart – God's approval is enough, and He will send encouragement in unexpected places.

Reflection

Have you ever felt disappointed when those closest to you didn't celebrate your dreams or accomplishments? How might God be using that silence to shift your focus back to His voice? Can you look back and see how He's used unexpected people to encourage you at just the right time?

Practical Step

This week, write down three Scriptures that remind you of your identity in Christ (example: Jeremiah 29:11, 1 Peter 2:9, Ephesians 2:10). Each time you feel unseen or unappreciated, read them aloud. Let God's Word drown out the silence of others.

Prayer

Father, when others don't see or celebrate me, help me remember that You do. Anchor my worth in Your voice alone, and give me strength to walk in the calling You've placed on my life. In Jesus' name, Amen.

With Love,
Heide Watson

Section 2

MERCY

Lessons, Growth,
and
God's Presece

Mercy is God's way of meeting us right where we are – whether in chaos, burnout, or loneliness – and reminding us that He hasn't left. His mercy slows us down when we're rushing, steadies us when we're overwhelmed, and opens our eyes to lessons we'd miss otherwise.

These devotionals step into the middle ground: not rock bottom anymore, but not fully healed either. It's the in between, where growth happens, where faith deepens, and where we begin to notice God's fingerprints on everyday life.

This section is about learning to walk with God – not just in desperation, but in daily moments of calm, kindness, and quiet transformation.

When We Seek God

My Story

I thought I understood what it meant to seek God – until He showed me again in a new way.

On my healing journey I began to have deeper thoughts and questions on life. I started to think about why is it that we cry out to God in times of struggle, but when life is good, we tend to "forget" Him or say we don't have time? I've noticed this pattern in my own life. I'll admit, I've been guilty of running closer to Him in hard times than in happy ones. But I'm working to change that, because I've learned something important: staying close to God in the good times is what helps carry us through the bad.

Think about it: when was the last time you prayed for someone who was doing well? Most of us say, "I'm praying for you" when someone is sick, struggling, or brokenhearted. But how powerful would it be if we also said, "I see you glowing, I see you thriving, and I'm praying for you"? Praying that God would continue blessing them, prospering them, and filling their life with joy. Happiness multiplies when we pray for it in others.

Sadly, most people look at the negative. The bad and the suffering. Years ago, a non-believer asked me, "If God is real, why does He allow bad things to happen to good people?" At first, I didn't know what to say. But then I realized: we are here on earth for God's purpose, not our own. Most of the time, we don't understand His purpose. But He is always working through it – even when it doesn't make sense to us.

I've seen countless videos of children fighting rare diseases or cancer—stories that break your heart to watch. I don't even know these families, yet their pain makes me cry. But I've also seen the way people rally together to surround them with prayer, support, and love. It's amazing how much unity and compassion can rise out of suffering.

If life were perfect—if everyone got everything they wanted—would we even seek God at all? Let's be honest. Most people forget Him when everything is going well. But in moments of desperation, we cry out, bargain, and plead: "God, if You do this for me, I promise I'll never…" I've been there. Maybe you have too.

"Sometimes the deepest struggles are the very moments God uses to draw others to Him."

That child fighting cancer, that family enduring pain— they often bring thousands of people closer to God through their story. Social media alone allows millions to witness, pray, and turn their hearts back to Him. Suffering often becomes the stage where God's glory shines the brightest.

No, it doesn't seem fair. No, it doesn't feel right. But God has a bigger plan. Those who suffer here will be rewarded in Heaven—a place free of pain, filled only with joy. That's why I stopped fearing death years ago. What we face on earth can't compare to the glory and peace waiting for us in Heaven. That's what I look forward to. Do you?

So I pray—for the families walking through fire, and for the people whose faith is being awakened by their stories.

I pray for healing, for strength, and for hearts to keep seeking Him.

And I remind myself daily: stay close to God in every season—not just in struggle, but in joy too.

Scripture says, "Rejoice always, pray continually, give thanks in all circumstances; for this is God's will for you in Christ Jesus." (1 Thessalonians 5:16–18).

The first time I heard this verse it stirred something in me, but this time it took on a whole new depth.

Don't wait for a storm to draw near to God—walk with Him in every season, in both struggle and joy.

Prayer

Father, forgive me for the times I only ran to You in desperation. Teach me to walk closely with You in the good and the bad, in joy and in sorrow. Help me to pray not only for those in struggle, but also for those who are thriving—that their joy would multiply and point others back to You. Keep my heart steady in every season. In Jesus' name, Amen.

When We Seek God

Devotional Guide

Scriptures:

1 Thessalonians 5:16–18

"Rejoice always, pray continually, give thanks in all circumstances; for this is God's will for you in Christ Jesus."

James 4:8
"Come near to God and He will come near to you."

Devotional

Why do we cry out to God when life hurts, but forget Him when life feels good? I'll admit, I'm guilty of it too. We usually offer prayers for people in crisis. But what about praying for people who are thriving? Imagine saying: "Lord, thank You for their joy. Keep blessing them. Keep multiplying their peace." Prayers like that make joy contagious.

The truth is, if life were perfect, most of us wouldn't seek God at all. Struggles often drive us to our knees. And yet, even suffering is used by Him for a greater purpose. That's why stories of children fighting illness can move millions of strangers to prayer—because even pain can point us to God.

No, suffering doesn't feel fair. But Heaven is coming, and it will be free of all pain. Until then, God asks us to walk closely with Him—not just in storms but in sunshine too.

Story

I remember praying endlessly for God to remove a struggle in my life. Years later, I realized that season taught me how to depend on Him more than ever before. Had everything been easy, I probably would've forgotten Him.

Takeaway Line

Don't just seek God in the storm—walk with Him in the sunshine, too.

Reflection

Do you seek God only in your struggles, or also in your seasons of joy?

Practical Step

Today, pray for someone who is thriving. Thank God for their joy and ask Him to keep blessing them.

Prayer

Father, draw me close to You not just when I'm desperate, but when I'm grateful too. Remind me to praise You in both pain and peace. Amen.

With Love,
Heide Watson

Slow Down

My Story

Rest wasn't a new lesson for me, but God brought it back again because I still hadn't mastered it.

I came across a video one afternoon that really spoke to me. Maybe these words will speak to you as well. The man in the video said he had a prophetic word for someone:

"You know it took Jesus 33 years to reach His destination… Why are you rushing to get to yours? Had Jesus been running, He would have passed by all the people who needed His blessing along the way. You'll never read about Jesus running anywhere. He understood how important the journey was. Stop rushing to get to your destination and fall in love with the people you meet along the journey. God said, 'There are so many people I want to bless through you, but at the speed you're going, you'll never see them. Slow down. Walk as Jesus did, and you'll get there sooner than you think.'"

What a perspective.

The video resonated with me because I knew it was true of my own life. I used to live in constant hurry. My calendar was always full, my to-do list never ended, and I wore my busyness like a badge of honor. I thought moving fast meant I was productive, successful, even spiritual. But in reality, I was missing so much.

I'll never forget one particular day when I was racing from one commitment to another. I stopped at a store to grab something quick, and a woman in one of the aisles struck up a small talk. My mind screamed, "I don't' have time for this." Afterwards, I rushed through the checkout and practically ran back to my car. But as soon as I shut the door, I felt the Holy Spirit whisper, "She needed more than your hurry. You missed her."

Since then, I've had multiple occasions this happened to me because I was in too big of a hurry. I don't even know their names, but I'll always wonder if they each just needed someone to look them in the eyes, slow down, listen, and care. To be honest, I've been in their shoes a time or two myself just wanting someone to listen or care and everyone is in too big of a rush.

It took me a long time to realize this myself. For years I rushed through life—always busy, always in a hurry—missing so much around me. Most of us do. We forget that the journey is the point: the lessons we learn, the people we meet, the love we discover, the experiences we share.

"The journey itself is where the blessings live."

Think about it—how often do we stop to notice the beauty God has surrounded us with? The people He's placed in our path? The small, ordinary moments that hold extraordinary meaning? Too often, we don't.

It's time to change that. Let's slow down. Let's walk as Jesus did—unhurried, intentional, fully present. Because when we do, we begin to see the blessings right in front of us. It actually brings a lot of happiness too.

"Let us fix our eyes on Jesus, the pioneer and perfecter of faith. For the joy set before him he endured the cross, scorning its shame, and sat down at the right hand of the throne of God." — Hebrews 12:2

Don't rush through life. Walk as Jesus did—slow, intentional, and present—so you don't miss the people and blessings along the way.

Prayer

Lord, forgive me for the times I've rushed through life, chasing the next milestone while missing the beauty of the moment. Teach me to slow down, to walk as Jesus did, and to see the people and blessings You've placed in my path. Help me to value the journey as much as the destination. In Jesus' name, Amen.

Slow Down

Devotional Guide

Scripture: Ecclesiastes 3:1

"There is a time for everything, and a season for every activity under the heavens."

Devotional

When was the last time you truly slowed down? Our culture glorifies hurry—fast goals, fast answers, fast everything. But Jesus never rushed. Not once.

Think about it: if Jesus had sprinted from one place to the next, He would've missed people who needed Him along the way. The woman at the well. The blind man. The children who ran to Him. His calm pace made room for connection.

In my own life, I've learned that rushing robs me of joy. When I slow down, I notice God's blessings in the small things—a smile, a sunset, a quiet moment.

Maybe God is whispering to you: "Stop hurrying. Walk with Me. I'll get you where you need to go."

Story

I once rushed through a season of my life so fast that I missed moments with people who mattered most. Looking back, I would trade every achievement for just one more slow dinner with them.

Takeaway Line

Life isn't about racing to the finish line, it's about who you notice along the way...

Reflection

What areas of your life are you rushing through instead of slowing down to notice God?

Practical Step

Schedule one "unhurried" moment this week—whether it's a walk, coffee with a friend, or just watching the sunset with no agenda.

Prayer

Lord, teach me to walk at Your pace. Slow my heart so I don't miss the people, lessons, and blessings You've placed along the way. Amen.

With Love,
Heide Watson

Changed Times

My Story

I'd seen how life changes before, but this season brought the truth home in a whole new way.

I often find myself thankful for the way I was raised. It wasn't just my parents who shaped me—it was an entire community. Some adults taught me respect, responsibility, and morals. Others, through their poor choices, showed me exactly what I didn't want in my life. Together, those lessons—both positive and negative— helped form who I am. And for that, I'm grateful.

When I think back to my childhood, I remember long country roads, wide open fields, and neighbors who were more like extended family. Everybody knew everybody. If you broke down on the side of the road, someone would stop to help. If you acted up, word got back to your parents before you walked through the door, or the neighbors had permission to treat you like they did their own child. Respect wasn't optional – it was expected.

Life feels different now. Sometimes I look around and wonder where that sense of honor and accountability went. I've overheard kids talk back to their parents in ways that would have never been tolerated when I was young. Respect, once a foundation, feels almost nonexistent. And that shift makes me wonder: what will life look like when our grandkids and great-grandkids grow up? Will they understand respect, kindness, and strong morals the way we once did? Or will those values fade into forgotten stories of the past?

That thought can feel heavy, but then I remember this truth: God's Word is not bound by culture or time. Scripture reminds us, "Train up a child in the way he should go; even when he is old he will not depart from it." (Proverbs 22:6, ESV).

I think back to the lessons I learned as a child—the Sunday mornings in church, the neighbors who stepped in with encouragement, the teachers who cared enough to set boundaries, even the discipline I didn't appreciate at the time. Those things stuck with me. They shaped my choices, my values, my view of the world. And even in seasons when I wandered, those foundations pulled me back to truth.

"Respect, once a foundation, feels almost nonexistent."

If that was true for me, it can be true for future generations too. God is still able to guide us back. He can remind us of who He created us to be and help us pass those values on to those who come after us. The world may change, but His Word never does.

"But as for you, continue in what you have learned and have firmly believed... from childhood you have been acquainted with the sacred writings, which are able to make you wise for salvation through faith in Christ Jesus." (2 Timothy 3:14–15).

The world's values may shift, but God's truth stands firm. And just as His Word anchors us through shifting times, He also grows us personally—teaching us to let go of what once mattered and embrace what really lasts. That's what I've been learning in my own life...

Prayer

Father, thank You for the people who shaped me, for the lessons that guided me, and even for the hardships that taught me what to avoid. As I look at the world today, I sometimes fear for the generations to come. But I choose to trust Your Word—that the seeds of truth planted in children will grow into a lifelong foundation. Help me to live as an example of respect, kindness, and faith, and to pass on values that last. In Jesus' name, Amen.

Changed Times

Devotional Guide

Scripture: Micah 6:8

"He has shown you, O mortal, what is good. And what does the Lord require of you? To act justly and to love mercy and to walk humbly with your God."

Devotional

Times have changed. Respect, kindness, and humility feel harder to find. The world seems louder, harsher, more self-centered.

But God's standard hasn't changed. He still calls us to live differently—to love mercy, act justly, and walk humbly. That hasn't gone out of style, even if the world thinks it has.

When I think back on my childhood, I'm thankful for the community of adults who raised me—not just parents, but teachers, neighbors, church members. Some taught me by example. Others taught me by showing me what not to do. Together, they shaped me.

Now it's our turn. What lessons are we leaving behind for the next generation? Are we showing our children what mercy looks like? Are we modeling humility? Or are we passing on selfishness and pride?

The times may change, but God's truth doesn't. Let's be the ones who carry it forward.

Story

Growing up, I remember neighbors looking out for each other. People waved, checked in, shared meals. Today it feels rare—but I've seen glimpses of it still alive when people choose kindness.

Takeaway Line

The world may change, but God's call to love and do what's right never does.

Reflection

What example are you leaving behind for the people watching your life?

Practical Step

This week, do one small act of kindness for someone without expecting anything back—just because it's the right thing to do.

Prayer

Father, help me to live with kindness, mercy, and humility in a world that desperately needs it. Let my life reflect Your goodness to others. Amen.

With Love,
Heide Watson

Be Calm

My Story

This wasn't the first time I had to learn to be calm, but it was the season where God made it real to me.

Life has a way of overwhelming us. The stress piles up, the phone keeps buzzing, and feels like we can't catch a break. I had a day where work was stressful, my phone wouldn't stop with calls and texts, bills were due, and on top of it all, friend drama was swirling in the background. I got home and climbed into bed immediately feeling like if one more thing got added to my plate, I was going to snap.

I remembered I had a guy friend who used to constantly tell me, "Be calm." Honestly, it drove me crazy. I always thought, "I am calm! If you want to see me not calm, I can show you!" But his words stuck in my head even as my chest tightened and my thoughts raced.

Over time, I realized what he meant wasn't just about my tone or attitude—it was about peace. Remaining calm even in the hard times. Stress didn't have to own me. Panic didn't have to be my default.

We can't go back and change the past. We can't control every outcome. But we can choose peace in the present moment. Accept what was. Focus on what is. Move forward.

And don't push away the people who bring calm into your life. You can't heal if you isolate and sulk. Pay attention to energy—it speaks louder than words. If someone gives you good vibes, stay close. If they bring negativity, protect your peace and walk away.

"Calmness isn't weakness—it's strength."

At the end of the day, you're the only one who controls how you respond to life. Calmness isn't pretending nothing is wrong. It's choosing not to let bad energy infect you.

That friend who used to tell me "Be calm" is still in my life today. And because of his constant reminders, I've learned to stay peaceful, to remove myself from negativity, and to stop letting other people's chaos dictate my mood.

Be calm. Trust God. Let go. Peace makes space for clarity.

Being calm about everything allows your mind to find solutions. Calmness is also a state of trust. Instead of overthinking and overreacting, you just surrender for that moment and allow yourself to receive guidance for what does not make sense.

"You will keep in perfect peace those whose minds are steadfast, because they trust in you." — Isaiah 26:3

Calmness is not weakness. It's trusting God enough to let go of control and walk in peace.

Prayer

Lord, thank You for being the source of my peace. Help me to stay calm when life feels chaotic and to trust You instead of reacting in fear. Surround me with people who bring peace and remove the influence of negativity from my heart. Teach me to rest in You, knowing You hold every outcome in Your hands. In Jesus' name, Amen.

Be Calm

Devotional Guide

Scripture: Philippians 4:7

"And the peace of God, which transcends all understanding, will guard your hearts and your minds in Christ Jesus."

Devotional

"Be calm." Those two words used to drive me crazy. I'd think, I AM calm! But looking back, I see what my friend meant. He wasn't telling me to lower my voice—he was pointing me toward peace.

We live in a world that thrives on chaos. Noise. Anger. Drama. If you aren't careful, you'll absorb all of it like a sponge. But peace—the kind only God gives—cuts through the noise. It keeps your heart steady even when life shakes.

Being calm isn't about ignoring problems. It's about responding instead of reacting. It's about stepping back, breathing, and remembering Who holds control. Pay attention to energy—yours and others. If someone lifts you up, draw closer. If someone drains your peace, step away.

Calm is strength. Calm is trust. Calm is surrendering control to the One who already has it.

Story

I remember a time when I was sitting in traffic, late for meeting a friend for dinner, and my anxiety was through the roof. My friend's words echoed in my head: "Be calm." At the time, I wanted to roll my eyes. But instead of snapping, I turned off the radio, took a deep breath, and whispered a prayer. The traffic didn't change, but something in me did. My heart slowed down. My thoughts settled. That's the difference God's peace makes—it changes us, even if the situation doesn't change.

Takeaway Line

Calmness isn't about the storm outside—it's about the anchor inside.

Reflection

Where in your life do you need to stop reacting and start resting in God's peace?

Practical Step

This week, choose one stressful moment—at work, in traffic, at home—and instead of reacting immediately, pause. Take one deep breath, whisper "Be calm, Lord," and let His peace meet you right there.

Prayer

Lord, teach me to stay calm when storms rise. Guard my heart and mind with Your peace, and help me choose trust over fear. Amen.

With Love,
Heide Watson

Kindness Is Rare, Cherish It

My Story

I'd seen this truth play out before, but God kept reminding me that kindness will always stand out.

Something I've been thinking about a lot lately: it's hard to find the same kindness you give reflected back to you. Over the years, I've seen this truth in relationships, conversations, and just watching people.

For me, kindness hasn't been about grand gestures – it's about showing up. I think back to the times I've quietly gone out of my way for others: showing up for ballgames for friends' children, spending hours on the phone listening to them talk about their problems, showing up when they needed someone to just be there, taking care of things behind the scenes so their load would feel lighter. I didn't do it for recognition; most people never even knew. But that's the thing about kindness – it's rarely loud. It's often the quietest gift.

And if I'm honest, sometimes it felt like nobody noticed. I poured out love, time, and energy, and in return, I felt I was overlooked or even taken for granted at times. That can sting. But it also made me realize something important: true kindness doesn't keep score. It doesn't give to get. It gives because that's who you are.

When I think of "kindhearted people," it's not the ones who do things to be noticed. I mean the quiet, genuine souls:

* The ones who smile and laugh easily.
* The ones who show up in times of need.
* The ones who calm you more than anyone else can.

* The ones who make you part of their family.
* The ones who sit with you in hospitals, cheer you on at ballgames, or pick up groceries so you don't have to.
* The ones who love children not biologically theirs, but theirs by choice of love.
* The ones who do all of this without complaint, without keeping score—simply because their heart overflows.

These are the truly kind people. And yet, too often, they're the ones who get overlooked, taken for granted, or even discarded. What should be cherished has become rare.

Scripture teaches us to be Christlike—to love unconditionally, forgive freely, give without expecting in return, and withhold judgment. And yet, just as many rejected Jesus in His time, people today still reject those with His kind of heart. They use them when it's convenient and cast them aside when it's not.

I can often spot a hurting soul by their eyes. They smile on the outside, but behind it is exhaustion—sometimes even depression. They keep pouring into others so no one else feels the pain they carry. And the world rarely notices.

"They smile on the outside, but behind their eyes is exhaustion no one notices."

That's why my prayer is that we wake up. That we learn to notice and value the Christlike hearts among us. That we make time for the people who make us smile, who show up, who bring light into our lives. Cherish them. Protect them. Because they are few and far between.

The world has grown harsh, but kindness still carries the power to change it. And it has to begin with me. With you. With all of us choosing to live it out.

As the saying goes: "I must be the change I wish to see in this world."

And Scripture says it this way: "Be kind and compassionate to one another, forgiving each other, just as in Christ God forgave you." (Ephesians 4:32).

Cherish the truly kind people in your life—and ask God to help you reflect that same Christlike kindness.

Prayer

Lord, thank You for the kindhearted people who reflect Your love in quiet, powerful ways. Forgive me for the times I've overlooked them or taken them for granted. Help me to notice, to cherish, and to protect those rare souls. And, Father, make me more like them—more like You. In Jesus' name, Amen.

Kindness Is Rare, Cherish It

Devotional Guide

Scripture: Ephesians 4:32

"Be kind and compassionate to one another, forgiving each other, just as in Christ God forgave you."

Devotional

Kindness feels rare these days. The world applauds ambition, competition, and self-promotion—but kindness? It often gets overlooked. Yet kindness is exactly what makes someone unforgettable.

Think about the people in your life who show up without being asked. The ones who cheer for you, sit with you in the hard times, or surprise you with small acts of love. They don't keep score. They don't demand anything in return. They just give because that's who they are.

These are the Christ-like hearts among us. But too often, they're taken for granted. Overlooked. Even discarded. Don't let that be you. Cherish the kindhearted people God places in your life. And better yet—be one of them.

Kindness may not make headlines, but it changes lives. And it reflects Jesus more than anything else we can offer.

Story

Some of the kindest people I know are the ones who've been hurt the most. They give without expecting anything back. And yet, they're often overlooked or taken for granted. Seeing this taught me never to waste genuine kindness—it's one of the rarest gifts in this world.

Takeaway Line

Kindness is holy ground—treat it like treasure when you find it.

Reflection

Do you take the kind people in your life for granted? Are you living in a way that reflects kindness to others?

Practical Step

Reach out to someone in your life who has shown you quiet kindness. Thank them specifically for what they've done.

Prayer

Lord, make me kind. Help me cherish those who pour love into my life and help me be the kind of person who does the same for others. Amen.

With Love,
Heide Watson

The Lonely Tree

My Story

There's a tree I pass almost every day on my drive to and from work. It sits alone on the side of the road, out in the open for everyone to see. Shaped a little oddly, set apart from the others—but still beautiful. If you're from my area, you probably know exactly which one I'm talking about. It's hard to miss.

This morning, the fog was heavy, and I couldn't resist snapping another picture. I already have dozens— sunrises, sunsets, each season bringing its own backdrop. And yet, every time, it takes my breath away.

That tree has become more than scenery to me—it's a daily reminder. Even when I feel alone or out of place, there is still beauty to be found. It stands out. It's strong. It's resilient. It may not look like the others, but it carries a beauty all its own.

I guess I connect with it because I've often felt the same way. Growing up, I was never the one who "fit in" easily. I wasn't the most popular, I didn't always wear the right clothes, and sometimes I just felt… different. I got along with everyone, I just didn't feel I had a place anywhere. Even as an adult, there have been seasons where I've walked into a room and thought, I don't belong here. I'm not like everyone else. It can feel isolating – like standing off to the side while everyone else is grouped together.

But over time, I've realized those moments didn't mean something was wrong with me. These were God's way of reminding me that I wasn't created to blend in – I was created to stand out. Just like that tree, I wasn't designed to be identical to anyone else. My story, my scars, my personality – they all carry a beauty that's unique to me.

"Its uniqueness is what makes it beautiful."

And maybe that's the reminder we all need: different isn't less. Different is what makes us shine.

Scripture says, "I praise you because I am fearfully and wonderfully made; your works are wonderful, I know that full well." (Psalm 139:14). God didn't design us to blend in. He designed us with unique fingerprints, stories, and purposes.

That tree stands tall through storms, seasons, and change. And so can we. Its beauty isn't found in looking like the others, but in simply being what it was created to be.

Don't hide what makes you different—embrace it. God created you to stand out for His glory.

Prayer

Father, thank You for creating me uniquely, with purpose and beauty. Help me to see myself through Your eyes and to embrace the differences that make me who I am. When I feel alone or out of place, remind me that I am never truly alone—I am Yours. In Jesus' name, Amen.

The Lonely Tree

Devotional Guide

Scripture: Isaiah 41:10

"So do not fear, for I am with you; do not be dismayed, for I am your God. I will strengthen you and help you; I will uphold you with my righteous right hand."

Devotional

On my daily drive to work, I pass a tree that stands all alone in an open field. It's oddly shaped, separated from the others, yet strikingly beautiful.

That tree reminds me of us. Sometimes we feel out of place, different, even lonely. But just like that tree, our uniqueness is what makes us beautiful. Our strength is often revealed when we stand alone.

God doesn't make mistakes. If you feel like you don't "fit in," maybe that's because you were meant to stand out.

Story

There's a tree I pass almost every day—standing all alone in an open field. It's oddly shaped, different, and separate from the others, yet it's beautiful in its own way. That tree reminds me that even when I feel out of place, God still sees me as strong, unique, and worth noticing.

Takeaway Line

Even when you feel alone, you're still rooted in God's strength and beauty.

Reflection

Where in my life do you feel "alone," and how might God be using that season to strengthen you?

Practical Step

The next time you feel out of place, step outside, and notice one part of creation that feels uniquely beautiful. Let it remind you of your own worth in God's eyes.

Prayer

Lord, when I feel alone, remind me You are always with me. Help me see beauty in my uniqueness and strength in my seasons of solitude. Amen.

With Love,
Heide Watson

Section 3
MIRACLES

Transformation,
Renewal,
and
Joy

The miracle isn't just that God rescues us from our darkest moments – it's that He changes us through them. The "new me" is healthier, lighter, happier, and more at peace because I've learned to surrender, to love myself as God created me, and to trust Him with my story.

These devotionals celebrate that transformation. They remind us that God doesn't just bring us through hard seasons – He brings us out stronger, wiser, and ready to shine His light into the world.

This section is about joy, hope, and rebirth. It's about realizing that every ending can become a new beginning, and every scar can tell the story of God's grace.

Love

My Story

God had spoken to me about love before, but He showed me once again how deep and unconditional it really is.

"Love is not what you say. Love is what you do. Every scar I have makes me who I am."

Ah, the big "L" word. Probably the most misused word in our vocabulary—and yet the one we crave the most. For years, I wrestled with what love really meant. I studied how people gave it, how they received it. I tried to find it in relationships, only to end up empty and depleted.

Here's the raw truth: I've been married multiple times, and I was the one who left. Not because I wanted to give up, but because I was unhappy – searching for something I couldn't seem to find. I thought love meant the butterflies, the passion, the feeling of being wanted. But every time the excitement faded and reality set in, I found myself thinking, this isn't it. This isn't enough. And I would convince myself that they were better off with someone else that would make them happy. Walking away only left me more aware of the emptiness inside.

It took me a long time to realize love doesn't begin with someone else. It begins with me.

For years, I sought love to feel whole, to feel like I mattered. Each relationship, each heartache left me disappointed—but also taught me something new. What I was searching for wasn't missing in other people. It was missing in me.

Eventually, I hit a season of depression, feeling unloved and unseen – even though I was the one who kept leaving. That's when I had to face the truth: no human being was ever going to fill what only God could.

"What I was searching for wasn't missing in other people. It was missing in me."

The real turning point came from an unexpected place: a TikTok video. (Yes, I'm a 40-year-old woman who loves TikTok—no shame!) It was a Pastor from Transformation Church. His message? Stop looking to people for love. Seek God first, because His love is unconditional. When we're full of His love, we stop chasing it in all the wrong places—and we begin to attract people who love us in truth.

That was my wake-up call. I already knew I could control my thoughts and feelings—but I needed the push. Once I started seeking God first, my whole view of love shifted. I began learning self-love—not conceit, but confidence in how God created me. If I couldn't love myself as He made me, I'd always be chasing a void only He could fill.

It sounds simple, doesn't it? And honestly—it is. But it requires a change in mindset. Start by focusing on the good in yourself. Stop picking yourself apart. Speak kindly to yourself. Laugh at yourself. Celebrate the way God made you unique.

Fall in love with you—because that's where true love begins.

"We love because He first loved us." — 1 John 4:19

True love doesn't begin with others. It begins with God's love in you—overflowing into the way you see yourself and the way you love others.

Prayer

Father, thank You for loving me with an everlasting love. Teach me to see myself through Your eyes and to stop chasing love in places it was never meant to be found. Help me to embrace self-love—not pride, but the confidence of knowing I am fearfully and wonderfully made. Let Your love fill every empty place in me, and may it overflow to those around me. In Jesus' name, Amen.

Love

Devotional Guide

Scripture: 1 John 4:19

"We love because He first loved us."

Devotional

"Love" is one of the most overused and misunderstood words in our vocabulary. (""Love is one of the most overused... - In Touch Ministries") We crave it, we chase it, and we try to define it in a thousand different ways. For years, I looked for love in other people—hoping someone could fill the emptiness inside me. But each time, I ended up more drained and disappointed.

Then I realized: love doesn't begin with others. It begins with God. He loved us first—long before we were worthy of it. And when His love fills us, it transforms how we see ourselves and how we love others.

The truth is you can't pour out what you don't have. Until we accept God's unconditional love and practice self-love through His eyes, we will always chase a broken version of it in others.

Loving yourself isn't selfish or vain. It's acknowledging the masterpiece God created when He made you. When you love yourself rightly, you are free to love others in a pure, healthy, and God-honoring way.

Story

For years, I chased love in all the wrong places— relationships, approval, attention. Each time, I ended up empty. The turning point came when I realized God's love had been with me all along, steady, and unconditional. That shift changed how I loved myself and how I could finally love others.

Takeaway Line

You can't pour real love into others until you've received God's love for yourself.

Reflection

Do you look for love in others before turning to God's love for you?

Practical Step

Write down three ways you can show love to yourself this week—through rest, encouragement, or simply speaking kind words over your life.

Prayer

Father, thank You for loving me first. Help me see myself the way You see me and teach me to love others from the overflow of Your love in me. Amen.

With Love,
Heide Watson

The Right Partner

My Story

> Choose a partner that is good for you.
> Not good for your parents. Not good
> for your image. Not good for your
> bank account. Someone who is
> making your life emotionally fulfilling.
> UNKNOWN | VIARESOURCE

I'd already wrestled with lessons on love, but God
brought this one back around in a new way.

When I look back on my younger years, I realize how
many times I got love wrong. I thought certain things
mattered—what someone had, how they looked, the
image they projected. And honestly, I fell for some of it.
But the older I get, the more I see how empty those things
really are.

I'll be honest: in my multiple marriages, I was the one
who left, and it wasn't because I didn't want love, but
because I was chasing a version of love that could never
satisfy. I thought security would come from money, or
that happiness would come from appearances. But once
the surface wore off, I realized those things couldn't
cover up the lack of peace underneath. I'd find myself
sitting in a pretty house or a nice car, yet feeling lonelier
than ever. It didn't matter what we owned if there was no
laughter, no prayer, no real connection.

That's when I learned firsthand: peace is far greater than chaos.

So many people believe money is the key to love. Others think it's status or appearance that makes someone desirable. But none of that lasts. Looks fade. Money comes and goes. And pretending to be "above" others by flashing wealth or image only leads to a mess.

"A man should have to find God before he finds your heart."

I remember listening to a sermon not long ago about relationships—whether starting fresh or strengthening the one you're in. The message was simple, but it hit home: put God first. If you're single, build your life with Him before anyone else. If you're married or dating, center your relationship on Him. That's the path to real peace.

Because the real questions in a relationship aren't about what's in the bank account or how good you look in photos together. They're these:

* Can you communicate honestly?
* Do you laugh and truly enjoy life together—or is it all for show?
* Do you share common values and interests?
* Do you pray together? Do you spend time with God together?

We should be paying attention to the little things. Watch how a person treats others, listen to the words that come out of their mouth, and notice where their priorities lie. You can only hide behind looks, money, or lies for so long—the truth will always come out.

If I'm honest, I wish I had learned these lessons earlier. My past relationships haven't always been smooth, and yes, I played a part in that too. But with time, growth, and

God's guidance, I've realized what really matters. And if sharing my story can help someone else avoid those same mistakes, then it's worth it.

So, be patient. Be real. Let love unfold naturally. Don't chase status or settle for chaos. Build on peace. Build on faith. And choose the right partner for the right reasons.

"Unless the Lord builds the house, those who build it labor in vain." — Psalm 127:1

Love that lasts is built on God's foundation—not money, looks, or status.

Prayer

Father, thank You for showing me what real love is. Forgive me for the times I've chased appearances instead of Your truth. Teach me to value character, peace, and faith above all else. If I am single, help me build my life with You first. If I am in a relationship, help me center it on You. May every connection I have reflect Your love. In Jesus' name, Amen.

The Right Partner

Devotional Guide

Scripture: Proverbs 18:22

"He who finds a wife finds what is good and receives favor from the Lord."

Devotional

Too often, we confuse love with looks, status, or money. But real love—the kind that builds a strong foundation—runs deeper than that.

Looks fade. Money comes and goes. Status can be stripped in a moment. But a heart that honors God, communicates with kindness, and chooses daily to love—that's what lasts.

When we put God first in our own lives, we begin to see relationships differently. We stop rushing. We start paying attention to character. We notice how someone treats others, whether they bring peace or chaos, whether they build up or tear down.

If you're single, trust God with your heart. Let Him write your story. If you're married, it's never too late to realign your relationship with Him. Pray together. Laugh together. Encourage one another. Put God first, and your partner second—and everything else will flow from there.

Story

I once thought a good relationship was built on looks or financial security. But when those faded, so did the connection. Over time, I discovered the deepest relationships are rooted in shared faith, peace, and laughter—the kind of bond that still feels light even in heavy seasons.

Takeaway Line

The right partner isn't found by chasing perfection—it's found by walking together toward God.

Reflection

Do your current or past relationships reflect God's love, peace, and purpose—or have they been built on temporary things?

Practical Step

If you're single, pray for God to prepare you and your future partner. If you're in a relationship, take 10 minutes today to pray together or share what you're most grateful for in each other.

Prayer

Lord, guide my relationships. Help me honor You in the way I love and be wise in choosing who I let close to my heart. Amen.

With Love,
Heide Watson

How Life Changes

My Story

God kept circling me back to the reality that life is always shifting – and His hand is steady through it all.

It's crazy how life changes as we get older. The things I once thought mattered—looks, status, career moves, even certain friendships—don't carry the same weight anymore. Back then, I believed I couldn't live without certain people or things. Looking back now, most of it feels so small.

I can still remember friendships in my younger years that I thought would last forever. A few almost lasted 40 years, others were much shorter. We did everything together – laughed, cried, stayed up too late talking about boys and dreams. But somewhere along the way, life shifted. People changed. Some grew distant, others took paths that didn't line up with mine, and suddenly those "forever" friendships faded into memories. At the time, it hurt. I wrestled with questions like, what did I do wrong? Why did things change?

But as the years went by, I realized something: not every friendship is meant to last a lifetime. Some are meant to teach us, shape us, and then release us. And that's okay.

With maturity comes perspective. These days, peace and happiness mean more than popularity or a crowd of people around me. Instead of chasing surface-level connections, I crave something deeper: real loyalty, shared values, and friends who lift me up in faith. Friends who bring out the best in me, who make me smile, laugh, and happy.

Every friendship I've had has been different, and I don't regret a single one. Each taught me something valuable. But the common denominator in them all was me – and for a long time, I didn't know what I truly wanted or needed from a friend. I thought having more friends meant I was more loved, but eventually I learned: it's not about quantity. It's about quality.

But I've learned one important truth: if the energy isn't right, I walk away. Life is too short to pour myself into what doesn't align with who God is shaping me to be.

These days, I treasure the rare souls who love with their whole hearts—the ones who show up, even when they're hurting. The ones who bend, sacrifice, and stay loyal. Those are the friends' worth holding close, the kind of love worth waiting for.

"Respect and loyalty may feel rare, but when you find them in a true friend, guard them like treasure."

Because true friendships aren't built on convenience or image. They're built on loyalty, prayer, encouragement, and joy. They're built when two people choose to put God first, and each other second – not on fairytales, but on raw, real love.

Life has a way of opening our eyes. What once seemed important now fades into the background, while what truly matters grows clearer every day. Scripture reminds us: "Above all, love each other deeply, because love covers over a multitude of sins." (1 Peter 4:8). That's the kind of love worth pursuing – in friendships, in family, and in every relationship we keep.

As I've grown, I've realized change isn't just something we see in relationships—it's written into every part of life. Seasons shift, friendships evolve, and God keeps teaching us through it all. Sometimes change hurts, but

like autumn leaves falling, it carries a hidden beauty.
Each ending holds the promise of a new beginning.

Prayer

Father, thank You for the friendships that have shaped me
– the ones that lasted, and even the ones that didn't.
Thank you for showing me that true friendship isn't about
how many people surround me, but about loyalty, prayer,
and love. Give me wisdom to value the right people,
courage to release the wrong ones, and grace to love them
all. In Jesus' name, Amen.

And just as friendships teach us about growth and
change, God also writes those lessons into creation itself.
Life's seasons are like the beauty of fall— they remind us
that with Him, every ending carries the promise of a new
beginning.

How Life Changes

Devotional Guide

Scripture: 1 Corinthians 13:11

"When I was a child, I talked like a child, I thought like a child, I reasoned like a child. When I became a man, I put the ways of childhood behind me."

Devotional

Isn't it funny how what we once thought mattered so much feels small now? The things we chased—status, approval, even shallow friendships—lose their shine with time.

As we grow older, peace becomes more important than drama. Depth matters more than appearances. Instead of chasing temporary highs, we crave lasting joy. Instead of surface-level attraction, we desire meaningful connection.

I've looked back on friendships and realized how much I didn't know about myself. I thought I needed certain things to be happy, but really, I just needed to understand who I was in Christ. Maturity shifts your perspective.

Now, I value people who bring peace into my life, who love without conditions, who encourage growth. I don't have the energy for chaos anymore—and honestly, that's a blessing. Life is too short to settle for anything less than love rooted in God's design.

Story

When I was younger, I thought what once mattered—looks, status, convivence, even the quantity of friendships mattered. When in reality true friendships aren't built on convenience or image or even quantity. They're built on loyalty, prayer, encouragement, and joy. They're built when two people choose to put God first, and each other second.

Takeaway Line

As we mature, our view of love and life matures too—it shifts from what excites us to what sustains us.

Reflection

How has your view of friendships shifted as you've matured in life and faith?

Practical Step

Take time this week to reflect on how your idea of love in friendships has changed over the years. Journal the traits you now value most in friendships.

Prayer

Father, thank You for showing me that real love grows deeper with maturity. Help me let go of what no longer matters and hold onto the friendships that reflect You. Amen.

With Love,
Heide Watson

Women Who Motivate Other Women

My Story

Encouragement has been a theme in my life, and God brought it back again through these women who lifted me up.

In March of 2020, right as the world shut down, I started a women's group on Facebook. None of us really knew what was happening. We were isolated, scared, and struggling. Personally, I was battling my own depression and insecurities. I didn't feel supported. I didn't feel accepted. I had hit rock bottom with all my mess going on in my life.

I knew there had to be other women going through similar things in life. I've heard similar stories through friends, coworkers, and even strangers. So, I knew I had to do something: I didn't want other women to feel the way I did. I wanted to create a space for encouragement, love, and support. I needed this too. At first, I felt like a hypocrite—posting uplifting quotes and prayers when my own heart was heavy. But something surprising happened. Those very posts began ministering to me too.

Again and again, the words I scheduled a month in advance to post for others were exactly what I needed to hear that day when they showed up. God has a way of working like that.

This group is to be a safe place for women, a place for positivity, a place to stop the mean girl mentality.

The "Mean Girl" mentality has become so awful in our world today. Not only do we see it as children in school, but it also occurs in adulthood. The truth is, we've all experienced the "mean girl" mentality one way or another. I've been judged, and I've judged. I've been hurt, and I've hurt others. But deep down, every woman I know just wants to be seen—for who she truly is. Most don't want to be a threat to each other. We want to be sisters.

That's why encouragement matters so much. When I compliment another woman, I can usually tell where she is in her confidence. If she brushes it off with, "I look awful," or "My hair's a mess," it tells me she hasn't felt beautiful in a long time. Somewhere along the way, another person likely tore her down. But when we speak life and love into women like this, something shifts. They begin to see the beauty God placed inside them.

Ladies, we need to stop the mean girl environment. Our daughters are watching. And if we don't model change now, they'll carry the same toxic cycles into adulthood. Instead, let's be hype women. Let's cheer each other on. Let's remind each other of our worth. Do away with jealousy.

"Let us not become conceited, provoking and envying each other." – Galatians 5:26

Here's a challenge: the next time you're with your friends and gossip comes up, pause. Ask yourself—do I really know her? Or am I just repeating what someone else said? More often than not, that woman is broken and needs encouragement, not judgment. Some of the best friendships I have today started with women others warned me about. When I actually took the time to know them, they were nothing like what I was told.

And if a woman truly isn't good for you, pray for her. Love her from a distance. But don't join the cycle of tearing her down. We never know when we might be the very person who inspires change in her life.

At the end of the day, God made us nurturers for a reason. We are meant to love, encourage, and lift each other up. That's why I started my group. If it only helps one woman change her mindset and feel loved, I've accomplished my mission.

Scripture says, "Therefore encourage one another and build each other up, just as in fact you are doing." (1 Thessalonians 5:11). That's the heart of it all.

And here's the beautiful part: when we begin to speak life into others, it doesn't just change them—it changes us. Loving others well flows out of loving ourselves the way God designed us. And when we remember that His love is the foundation, we find the courage to cheer on other women without insecurity or comparison.

Your words hold power—use them to build women up, not tear them down.

Prayer

Lord, thank You for the gift of sisterhood. Forgive me for the times I've judged or spoken words that tear others down. Help me to be a woman who encourages, uplifts, and protects the hearts of those around me. Let my words reflect Your love so that others can see their worth in You. In Jesus' name, Amen.

I invite you to join us on this journey. If my Facebook group only helps one woman change her mindset, I feel I accomplished a goal of mine in life. That is what it's all about to me.

Women Who Motivate Other Women

Devotional Guide

Scripture: Proverbs 31:26

"She speaks with wisdom, and faithful instruction is on her tongue."

Devotional

In 2020, during one of the hardest seasons of my life, I created a women's group on Facebook. At first, I felt like a hypocrite posting encouragement when I was struggling myself. But God used it—not just to encourage others, but to heal me too.

Women need women. We need each other's encouragement, prayers, and support. Yet too often, we see competition instead of compassion. Gossip instead of grace. Judgment instead of love.

I want to change that. I want women to know they are not alone. That there are women who will cheer them on, pray with them, and remind them they're beautiful inside and out.

Ladies, we were created to nurture and to uplift. When we choose encouragement over envy, we reflect the heart of God to each other.

Story

When I started my women's group in 2020, I felt unqualified. I was struggling myself. But the more I encouraged others, the more I realized God was using that same encouragement to heal me too. Supporting women taught me that we rise by lifting each other.

Takeaway Line

Strong women build each other up—they don't compete, they complete.

Reflection

Are you a woman who uplifts other women—or tears them down?

Practical Step

Send a message of encouragement to another woman today. Tell her one thing you admire about her.

Prayer

God, help me use my words to encourage and uplift. Heal the broken places in me so I can build others up, not tear them down. Amen.

With Love,
Heide Watson

Perception – Seeing Beauty from a Different Angle

My Story

"It's not strength, it's PERCEPTION that makes you stronger. If you change how you SEE it, you'll change how you FEEL about it." – Yvonne Pierre

I have a favorite tree as I have spoken about in other writings of mine. Anyone who knows me well has probably seen it plastered across my social media. I love everything about it.

The other night, I had to take a detour home because of roadwork, which put me right back in front of my tree. At first, I thought, "Well… not a great view today." There was no sunset, no glowing colors—just an ordinary backdrop. Still, I snapped a quick picture.

As I passed by, something caught my eye in the side mirror. I gasped, pulled over, spun the car around, and snapped another shot. What a difference!

That's when it hit me: perception.

It was almost like God whispered, "Look again." The very same tree, but from a different angle, carried an entirely new beauty.

"Change how you see it, and you'll change how you feel about it."

I started thinking about how often I've written something off in life because of how I initially saw it—or worse, because of how someone else told me to see it. But when I shifted perspective, what once seemed ordinary or disappointing suddenly carried beauty, value, and meaning.

Life is tough. We all face heartache, battles, and moments when we want to give up. I've been there too—fighting demons, walking through storms. But over time, I've learned the power of changing my perception. Instead of seeing challenges as punishment, I began asking: What can I learn from this? How can this grow me?

That shift changed everything. I became truly happy—not because life became easy, but because I saw life differently. I started surrounding myself with people who lifted my energy and letting go of those who drained it. I hear people say, "You look so happy. I love seeing you this way." And it's true—I am. Because my mindset finally changed.

Here's the thing: negative thinking attracts negative outcomes. Positive thinking? It opens the door to joy. No, we can't be "positive Annie" 24/7—that's not realistic. But we can practice catching ourselves when negativity creeps in, then shifting focus toward the good. Little by little, life feels lighter.

When I look at those two photos of my tree, taken minutes apart, I see beauty in both. One felt flat at first.

The other made me say "Wow." Same tree, same day—just seen from a different angle.

That's life. Change how you see it, and you'll change how you feel about it.

"Do not be conformed to this world, but be transformed by the renewal of your mind, that by testing you may discern what is the will of God—what is good and acceptable and perfect." — Romans 12:2

Your situation may not change, but your perspective can. And when your perspective changes, so does your peace.

Prayer

Lord, thank You for the reminder that perception matters. Help me to see situations through Your eyes and not just my own. When negativity tries to cloud my view, teach me to shift my perspective toward the lessons, blessings, and beauty You've placed in front of me. Renew my mind daily, and let me walk in peace and joy. In Jesus' name, Amen.

Perception – Seeing Beauty from a Different Angle

Devotional Guide

Scripture: 2 Corinthians 4:18

"So, we fix our eyes not on what is seen, but on what is unseen, since what is seen is temporary, but what is unseen is eternal."

Devotional

One evening, I stopped to take a photo of my favorite tree. At first, the view looked dull—no sunset, no vibrant colors. But then I looked again, from a different angle, and it took my breath away.

Life works the same way. Sometimes all we see is the pain, the disappointment, the "bad angle." But if we shift our perspective—even slightly—we can often find beauty, lessons, and growth.

Changing how we see changes how we feel. What once felt hopeless can become a source of strength.

Story

One evening, I drove past my favorite tree and thought it looked plain. But when I glanced in my mirror, I saw the same tree against a breathtaking backdrop. Same tree, different angle. It reminded me that so much in life depends on how we choose to see it.

Takeaway Line

Change how you see it, and you'll change how you feel about it.

Reflection

Are you focusing only on the "bad angles" in your life—or are you open to seeing God's beauty from a new perspective?

Practical Step

This week, take one situation you've labeled as "bad" and ask: "What might God be teaching me here?" Write down one possible blessing in disguise.

Prayer

Father, open my eyes to see Your hand in every situation. Help me shift my perspective from despair to hope, from fear to faith. Amen.

With Love,
Heide Watson

Making a Difference (Drive-Thru Story)

My Story

"You make an impact on the world around you every single day. Whether it's how you treat the tired grocery clerk or how you react to the rushed person who cut you off, you always send your energy into the world. When you call or do not call your momma, when you help or don't help someone pick up their dropped things, you are making an impact. And what's often forgotten is that the little impacts we make every day on our world are actually quite the opposite; they are not little at all, they are the acts that make the biggest difference." – Walk the Earth

I love this quote—it's so true.

Years ago, I was sitting in a drive-thru, waiting my turn to order. The woman taking orders sounded irritated and worn out, probably from dealing with a long line of impatient customers. You can always tell by their voice on the intercom what kind of day they are having by their tone. In that moment, I thought to myself, I bet she doesn't hear many "thank-you's" or feel much appreciation at all.

Right then, I made a choice: every time I go through, I'm going to be intentional with kindness. From that day on, I started saying, "Yes, ma'am" or "Yes, sir," and I always ended with a genuine, "Thank you."

You wouldn't believe how much it changes their demeanor. There's one local restaurant where a particular lady even recognizes my voice the moment I start ordering and by the time I get to the window, she's all smiles and warmth. All of that—just from something as simple as speaking kindly.

"Small acts of kindness are never small; they can change someone's entire day."

That little gesture has reminded me again and again how powerful small acts of kindness really are. We don't need a stage, a title, or a platform to make a difference. We already have the tools to brighten someone's day—we just need to use them.

Scripture says, "Do not withhold good from those to whom it is due, when it is in your power to act." (Proverbs 3:27). Every smile, every thank-you, every act of respect—it all matters. And those "little things" aren't little at all. They're the things that can change someone's entire day.

So next time, slow down. Adjust your attitude. Smile. Say thank you. You never know… you might be the one person who lifts someone's spirit when they need it most.

Small acts of kindness carry the biggest impact.

Now that is making a difference.

Prayer

Lord, thank You for reminding me that kindness is never wasted. Teach me to notice the people around me—the tired worker, the overwhelmed friend, the stranger carrying hidden burdens. Help me to speak life, to show respect, and to use my words and actions to reflect Your love. In Jesus' name, Amen.

Making a Difference (Drive-Thru Story)

Devotional Guide

Scripture: Matthew 5:16

"In the same way, let your light shine before others, that they may see your good deeds and glorify your Father in heaven."

Devotional

Years ago, I noticed a woman working in a drive-thru who looked tired and irritated. When I reached the window, I decided to simply say, "Thank you." Her entire demeanor shifted.

Since then, I make it a habit to say, "thank you" and show kindness in those small moments. It's amazing how one small gesture can brighten someone's entire day.

We often underestimate the impact of our words. But light shines brightest in small, simple acts of kindness.

Story

Years ago, I decided to always thank the workers at my local drive-thru. One woman who once seemed irritated now lights up when she hears my voice through the speaker. A simple "thank you" changed her whole demeanor—and mine too.

Takeaway Line

Small gestures of kindness can shine the brightest light.

Reflection

When was the last time you chose kindness in an ordinary moment?

Practical Step

Pick one everyday encounter—grocery clerk, waiter, mail carrier—and intentionally speak encouragement into their day.

Prayer

Lord, remind me that even small acts of kindness can glorify You. Help me use my words to spread light wherever I go. Amen.

With Love,
Heide Watson

Change

My Story

"My Favorite Time of Year"

Life reminds me often that growth and change are constant. Relationships shift, priorities realign, and even my perspective on love has matured over time. But it's not just people who teach us this truth—God has written it into creation itself. That's why fall has always been my favorite season…

There was a time when life felt like one long, heavy season. I smiled on the outside, but inside I was crumbling. My mind was weighed down with self-doubt, fear, and the feeling that I wasn't enough. I compared myself to everyone around me, constantly coming short. I poured myself out for others until there was nothing left of me, and I didn't know how to stop.

I tried to push through it. To be strong. To make things look good on the surface. Buth the truth is, I was exhausted. Spiritually dry. Mentally drained. And quietly asking myself if this was all life would ever be. It was at those lowest moments that God began to whisper to me "Let go. Give it to Me."

And little by little, I did. Like leaves falling one by one in the fall, God peeled away what no longer served me – my unhealthy habits, my toxic way of thinking, my need to control everything. It wasn't instant. Some days, I fought Him. Some days, I clung to the very things He was asking me to release. But the more I let go, the lighter I became.

Through the seasons of my life – spring's new beginnings, summer's joy, fall's letting go, winter's stillness – I've learned that change is not my enemy. It's God's way of making me new.

And slowly, I began to notice the difference. My mind was healthier. My heart was lighter. I could breathe again. I wasn't drowning in negativity or fear. I laughed more. I noticed the beauty around me. I felt free.

But more than anything, I grew closer to God. He stopped being an idea I ran to when life fell apart, and He became the steady presence I leaned on every single day. Prayer became my oxygen. His Word became my anchor. And His love became the lens through which I began to see myself.

Looking back now, I see it clearly: I am not the same woman I used to be. I am stronger. I am more at peace. I am learning to love myself as God created me. And I am finally happy – not because everything is perfect, but because I know Who is carrying me through every season.

"Even the dying leaves remind us that change is coming."

So, when I watch the leaves turn brilliant shades of red and gold, I see more than beauty. I see my own story written across the branches. I see how God used every ending to bring a new beginning. I see that rebirth is not just possible – its's His promise.

Scripture says, "See, I am doing a new thing! Now it springs up; do you not perceive it?" (Isaiah 43:19). And I do see it now – because I am living it.

Seasons change, and so do we. And with God, every ending carries the hope of something better ahead.

Prayer

Lord, thank You for carrying me through every season of my life. Thank You for the moment that broke me and the moments that healed me, because through both, You shaped me into someone new. Keep teaching me to let go of what no longer serves me, to embrace the growth You're calling me to, and to walk boldly in the joy and peace only You can give. In Jesus' name, Amen.

Change

Devotional Guide

Scripture: Ecclesiastes 3:1

"There is a time for everything, and a season for every activity under the heavens."

Devotional

Change is hard. It forces us to let go of comfort, to step into the unknown. But change is also where growth happens.

Think about the leaves in fall. They wither and die, yet even in their dying, they're beautiful. And soon after, new life begins again.

The same is true for us. Seasons of loss, endings, or transitions can feel painful, but they often bring rebirth and renewal. God never wastes a season.

Story

Fall is my favorite season because it reminds me that even dying leaves can be beautiful. Their colors signal that change is coming, that a new season is on its way. In the same way, even painful endings can hold beauty when God is bringing us into something new.

Takeaway Line

Change may feel like loss, but with God it's always a doorway to renewal.

Reflection

What season of change are you resisting, and how might God be using it to bring renewal?

Practical Step

Write down one change in your life that once hurt but later proved to be good. Thank God for how He used it to grow you.

Prayer

Father, help me trust You in seasons of change. Remind me that endings are often beginnings, and that You make all things new. Amen.

With Love,
Heide Watson

The Simple Things (Sunrises & Sunsets)

My Story

I've noticed something about myself: when I see something beautiful, I stop. Sometimes I even pull the car over just to take it in and snap a picture of the sunset or scenery. It might be a burst of colors splashed across the sky at sunset, or the quiet stillness of a field with fireflies glowing. It doesn't have to be big or fancy – it's the small things, the simple things, that bring me joy.

But if I'm honest, I didn't always notice them. Life has a way of pulling my attention to what I don't have, to the things I wish were different, or to the chaos pressing in. And when that happens, I miss what God is showing me right in front of my face.

The truth is, every single day we're surrounded by reminders of His goodness. The heavens are God's canvas, and each sunrise and sunset is a fresh stroke of His paintbrush. They're His way of whispering "I'm here. I'm still with you."

It's no accident that the day begins and ends with those moments. It's as if God is bookending our lives with beauty, saying: Start with Me. End with Me. Trust Me in between.

Scripture says it best: "The heavens declare the glory of God; the skies proclaim the work of his hands." (Psalm 19:1). The world around us is more than scenery—it's a living reminder that He hasn't forgotten us.

So maybe today, before you rush past, pause. Look up. Take in the sky, the breeze, the colors, the gifts He's already placed in your path. Appreciation grows not when we get more, but when we notice what we already have.

Prayer

Father, thank You for the beauty You've surrounded me with. Forgive me for the times I'm too busy or distracted to notice. Teach me to slow down, to see Your fingerprints in the simple things, and to let them remind me of Your faithfulness. May every sunrise and sunset be a call to trust You more. In Jesus' name, Amen.

The Simple Things (Sunrises & Sunsets)

Devotional Guide

Scripture: Psalm 19:1

"The heavens declare the glory of God; the skies proclaim the work of His hands."

Devotional

I'm the kind of person who will stop the car to take a photo of a sunset. Simple things like that bring me joy. But too often, we overlook them because we're focused on what we don't have.

God paints beauty around us every single day. Sunrises, sunsets, the stars at night—reminders of His presence and His power. These small gifts remind us: life is bigger than our problems.

Slow down. Look up. Appreciate the now. God is speaking through His creation every day.

Story

I love pulling over to snap pictures of sunsets and sunrises. They remind me of God's artistry—the promise of a new beginning each morning and the peace of an ending each night. The simple things carry the deepest truth if we just pause to notice them.

Takeaway Line

Gratitude grows when we learn to see God's beauty in the simple things.

Reflection

Do you take time to notice and thank God for the beauty around you?

Practical Step

Take five minutes this week to sit in silence outdoors—watching the sky, listening to the wind, or noticing the details of creation. Thank God for the gift of the present moment.

Prayer

Lord, open my eyes to the beauty You've placed in my life. Teach me to find joy in the simple things and to remember Your presence daily. Amen.

With Love,
Heide Watson

As you've walked through these pages, I hope you've seen the thread that runs through every story: we all face the **Mess**: those hard, confusing, painful seasons that test us. Yet in every mess, God shows His **Mercy** – offering lessons, healing, and the quiet reminder that He never leaves us. And through His mercy, He brings the **Miracles** – a renewed heart, a healthier mind, and the joy of becoming who He created us to be.

My story is still unfolding, and so is yours. None of us have "arrived." We're all learning, growing, and trusting God with the next step. But here's the truth you can carry with you: **with Him, no season is wasted. No wound is beyond healing. No past mistake is too big for His grace.**

So, wherever you find yourself today – whether deep in the mess, walking through mercy, or celebrating the miracles - remember this: **God is with you. He is working in ways you may not see yet, and He has a plan for your life that is far greater than anything you could imagine.**

Your past doesn't define you. Your present doesn't limit you. Your future is secure in His hands.

Hold onto hope. Keep walking forward. And trust that the same God who brought beauty out of my brokenness will do the same for you.

With love and faith,
Heide Watson

www.ingramcontent.com/pod-product-compliance
Lightning Source LLC
Chambersburg PA
CBHW050445150626
46551CB00028B/1683